# ANSILY TULENSRU

# Discovering your Why?

## Empath's guide to Self-Discovery

This book was professionally typeset on Reedsy.
Find out more at reedsy.com

# Contents

# Acknowledgement

I have had many people love and encourage me through this journey of life. Far too many to name; but know that I am grateful. I would like to take a moment to recognize a few that specifically helped me in learning about the meaning of being an empath. Perhaps, some of the best teachings, I have received about the gift of empathy are from the works and efforts of fellow empaths I've never had the opportunity to meet. The work and research of Dr. Judith Orloff, has especially been a great influence and personal source of encouragement for me. I'd also like to acknowledge Author and Life Coach Fraya Mortensen, of the Facebook group, The Evolving Empath, for her work and encouragement she freely offers. Their works as well as others all made this book possible.

Thank you

# Introduction: My why

My journey to self discovery began when I was seventeen. I have always felt out of place, as if something that made me me was simply off, or possibly broken. I obviously was not like everyone else. I am shy and an introvert and for a time I tried to rationalize my struggle with anxiety and depression with such labels. As I continued to struggle to find my place I realized I desperately wanted to discover that niche to which I belonged.

I would often try to just get through the day like a "normal" person and just do what I was supposed to do. Attend class, show up to work, get from point A to point B with as little interaction with the surrounding world as possible. My struggle with anxiety and depression reached a new low; obviously just doing what was expected didn't alleviate any of my problems and it certainly didn't bring me any sense of purpose or satisfaction. I decided I needed more help and that I wasn't able to fix myself by myself.

My mind often felt like a minefield of questions: Why? Why am I so different? Why can't I find my purpose? Why do I feel lost? And just why am I here? There were so many questions that I just wanted answers to. I wanted to know the why; I wanted to know my why; my reason for living and continuing to persevere. I struggled with every normal interaction there was. My constant anxiety spiraled me into a very dark place, a place I knew I couldn't dig myself out of. As I began to see a counselor, we worked on building awareness of possible triggers and uncovering their root causes. The work was hard and painfully slow. In addition, having to communicate the ins and outs of each day felt like just another job to add to my already hectic schedule.

Sometimes I felt as though searching for answers was a pointless struggle. I was so tired and finding purpose was a desire, however, survival was usually all I could manage. Mental, physical, and emotional exhaustion was my normal. I continued counseling and the tools and exercises given to me often seemed impossible to complete. I was missing something but I couldn't figure out what. I believe most people and possibly a more sensible person would have given up and either been complacent in continuing to cope, or abandon all hope. Fortunately, I am not like most people, I continued to do what I was supposed to do and find the tools necessary to overcome the constant stress and troubles life brought my way.

My journey began over twenty years ago and I have learned a great deal. I had to struggle through a lot of it and I often wished there was someone or something with answers, or at least an easier way. I wish that someone would have shared with me years ago what I intend on sharing in this book. Perhaps this will save others some of the time and frustration that I expended along my journey.

My normal was very different from the "normal" that other people would experience in their day to day life. I would often have bizarre encounters with strangers when I was just trying to get through the day; this was often draining and reinforced my belief that there was something essentially wrong with me. Trying to find the humor in things I would often entertain close friends with the retelling of these interludes. However, as these encounters became more and more frequent, I began to avoid any type of social event and became very withdrawn. Although I could find humor in these stories after the fact, each experience was unnerving and occasionally frightening. I didn't understand what it was about me that drew these people in. I am like a weirdo-magnet. I realize now that the very answer to this was the key I needed to make sense of these encounters and begin to effectively identify and remove barriers to personal growth and understanding.

The underlying reason I avoided crowds, attracted hurting and often broken people, or had unexplainable emotional responses or even why I am able to distinguish when someone is being truthful or not could all be explained by being an empath. When I first heard the term empath I admittedly assumed that it was a part of mysticism and I wasn't interested in that. However, as I learned that it had more to do with how I received and processed information I began to be more open to what it might mean to be an empath. This discovery has led me on a path of understanding that has made the biggest difference in my life. Learning about empaths has allowed me to better understand myself and the world around me. I have discovered that I am passionate about encouraging others and lifting them out of their own darkness. I hope that the lessons I've learned and share will help others discover why they are the way they are as well as uncover their "why" for existing. I would like to help others avoid the frustration and help them discover and pursue their own passions.This book is a condensed collection of information and experience to help other empaths or highly sensitive people learn about their unique gifting and the necessary skills needed to begin to thrive.

# The Basics

Empathy is an attribute that many of us value in others. The aspect that is attractive about empathy is understanding. If another person understands what we are personally going through then there is a sense of relief that our human experience is somehow validated. The ability to not only sympathize with another but to feel as the other is feeling can be difficult to comprehend; however, there are many that are so naturally predisposed to this that they are unaware that they are even experiencing another person's emotions. This sensitivity can manifest so seamlessly in one's personality that it is often misinterpreted by both the individual and others as a personality quark or deficiency.

Campbell, from Verywell Mind, defines an empath as a person highly attuned to the feelings and emotions of those around them (Campbell, 2022). She continues that:

Empaths feel what another person is feeling at a deep emotional level. Their ability to discern what others are feeling goes beyond sympathy, which is defined simply as the ability to understand the feelings of others. Instead, being an empath extends to actually taking those feelings on. (Campbell, 2022)

In addition, according to Garis, of Well + Good, there are eight types of empaths and only two of them relate to absorbing the energy from surrounding people. Apart from being interesting this further demonstrates how the understanding of an empath is expanding. However, so much more needs to be studied and uncovered. Psychiatrist, Judith Orloff, MD, is credited with documenting and explaining these eight types of empaths and has categorized them as follows: physical empath, emotional empath, intuitive empath, dream empath, plant empath and earth empath. Each type of empath has similar attributes but each subset has specific sensitivities that uniquely tune them into the word around them. You can learn more about each of these types of empaths in Orloff's book *The Empath's Survival Guide: Life Strategies for Sensitive People*. It would seem that the available information on being an empath continues to grow. (Garis, 2020)

Currently there is more awareness and understanding of how a young empathy or highly sensitive child may act, compared to their peers, but many are still mislabeled as difficult, overly sensitive, socially awkward or inept, or even believed to be on the spectrum of Autism. According to Psychologist Dr. Elaine Aron, who coined the term, "the highly sensitive child," high sensitivity is quite common. An estimated 15-20% of the population is considered to be of high sensitivity. Aron notes that high sensitivity has been studied in infants and children for over fifty years, however, due to the commonality of misunderstandings these studies were studied under different terms. Aron claims that highly sensitive children are often misunderstood and misjudged. Studies that included these children included studies on low sensory thresholds, shyness, introversion, fear, inhibition or timidness. All common attributes of the highly sensitive or empathic child. Sadly these attributes can often lead people to believe that the highly sensitive child is suffering from a disorder or illness when in reality it is nothing more than a personality trait, or processing preset. (Li, 2022)

Although the field of science, as a whole, does not agree on the existence of empaths, recent studies have found "mirror neurons" in the brain, these neurons may help us mirror the emotions of those we come in contact with. Preliminary results of this research shows that some people may have more mirror neurons than others; allowing me to conclude that not only is there the possibility that empaths "exist," but that there may soon be measurable scientific data for determining the degree and level at which an empath operates. (Campbell, 2022)

Because most Empaths are initially unaware of their unique wiring and why they are the way they are, they often internalize blame and feel responsible for the awkward or unusual socializing. For a person so attune with other people's feelings and emotions it can be hard for them to decipher their own feelings. An empath often feels as if there is something essentially wrong with them. As children, empaths often feel out of place or lost. These feelings can be carried into adulthood and without the proper skills necessary to shield an empath's energy and utilize their gifting, their struggle to make sense of the world will continue to be compounded.

Empaths or the highly sensitive are naturally deep thinkers and many of these feelings and misbeliefs developed in childhood can continue to confound and bemuse an empath. Dr. Orloff explains that when overwhelmed an empath can suffer from panic attacks, depression, chronic fatigue, food, sex and drug binges, and many physical symptoms

(Orloff, n.d.).  Conversely, studies have also shown that sensitive children thrive more than non-sensitive children when their childhood experiences are positive and their gifting allowed to mature (Li,2022). Essentially the misunderstood and unsupported empath may develop significant psychological, emotional, and physical problems while an empath allowed to work through and discover their gifting will often thrive and experience more success when compared to their peers.

Contrary to the nature of empathy an empath may struggle with understanding their own feelings and purpose. Absorbing surrounding energy from others, an empath, can easily mistake another person's emotions and feelings as their own.  Furthermore, internalizing the misunderstanding of labels such as being shy, introverted, reserved, or easily overwhelmed an empath can experience sensory overload. Although this is not necessarily a guaranteed experience of the empath, it is easy to see how one may enter adolescence and adulthood feeling broken.  Even so an empath is able to overcome these feelings of brokenness and confusion by familiarizing themselves with the gift of empathy and developing skills to utilize and nurture this gift.

# *What is the difference?*

Wired differently than an estimated 80% of the population the differences in how an empath receives and processes information can actually give them a competitive edge. Highly sensitive people have a more sensitive nervous system. Resulting in faster reflexes as well as sensitivity to pain, medications, and allergens. Their body is literally designed to perceive and comprehend anything they come across. This can allow an empath to be an effective First-Responder, or an asset in an emergency situation. They are often good at assessing data and applying it in a meaningful way. Empaths are amazing problem solvers, finding and addressing core issues or problems and finding solutions is almost effortless. An empath's gift makes an impact and meaningful difference in the world every day. (Li, 2022)

As to be expected there are both pros and cons to being an empath. Campbell lists that:

*empaths can provide emotional support for others, identify when someone is in need of help and tell if someone would be good for them. (Campbell, 2022)*

Campbell also lists some of the drawbacks which include:

> *often being too busy, feeling emotionally drained, and others may be reactive towards them when they feel the empath's observations are intrusive. It is often difficult for a highly sensitive person to find balance. Empaths often struggle with sleep and maintaining their mental health. (Campbell, 2022)*

The outside pressures of parents, teachers, friends, and society can make an empath feel like their very soul is being crushed or torn apart. Unable to establish their own feelings from what they're drawing in from the world functioning around them, an empath can struggle to find direction or purpose. As they absorb the information coming to them the messages they receive are often conflicting. An empath often makes decisions to please others that they feel closest to instead of discovering what they may want for themselves. It is easy for an empath to fall within the trap of believing that their purpose and meaning in life is to serve another's needs and desires.

Perhaps the hardest thing for an empath is to break free from an established toxic relationship. However separating themselves from such people is essential in defining themselves. Toxic people include anyone that they find draining. The level and severity of toxicity of others varies greatly and often creating space from these individuals feels selfish and almost unnatural for an empath.

Depending on the type of relationship and the severity of toxicity the action needed to separate oneself varies. Sometimes stating, "I am sorry, I can't, I need to take some time and space for myself," is all that is needed to establish space. Sometimes drastic measures need to be taken. The difficult decisions of moving out, changing jobs, changing numbers, or even getting a restraining order are hard choices but may be required to break free.

Establishing space is needed for an empath to begin to sort out their own emotions. Creating space may require a great deal of effort, creativity, and determination. Choosing to break free and prioritize their own well being is incredibly hard for an empath. Time may be needed to recover from creating this space and that is not only okay but to be expected. Time can be our greatest ally in healing.

Once alone, an empath can allow their own thoughts and feelings to surface. Finally discovering the difference between their own emotions and others. Using tools like journaling or mindfulness can streamline this process. One of the many benefits of being an empath are their instincts. An empath has the ability to ask themselves the right questions. Furthermore making the right decision is practically innate. However, it is not unusual for an empath just learning about their gift to struggle in this area. If an empath is still very drained or the feelings of guilt block this ability, assistance may be needed.

Reaching out and asking for someone to guide them through exploring and defining their feelings is greatly encouraged. Counselors, Psychiatrists, and Ministers are all trained in helping people sort out problems, offer suggestions, instruct and equip people with emotional tools as well as ask questions needed to help a person discern how they feel. It is important to find the right fit but the journey can continue even if the empath feels stuck and unable to sort things out for themselves. One should never feel guilty or uneasy about using their resources, people need one another and sometimes people need to be needed. Continuing the journey is what is important, not the resources used along the way.

# Tools for Protecting an Empath's Energy

An empath needs to learn how to tune into their gifting as well as learn how to protect it. Empaths naturally exchange energy with those around them. To a sensitive person, group settings, large social gatherings, or crowded events are often overwhelming (Campbell, 2022). This is an essential aspect of being an empath but without the skills necessary to shield their energy an empath is prone to exhaustion and fatigue. An empath may feel the need to withdraw or avoid people but obviously that is not realistic for every situation, nor is it a long term solution. Equipping an empath with some tools to shield or create a barrier between their energy and others is far more practical.

An empath needs to protect their energy from a world ready and willing to drain them of their gift. Dr. Orloff's blog post, *5 Protection Strategies for Empaths*, outlines how an empath can use Shielding Visualization to protect their energy and block out toxic energy (n.d.). Dr. Orloff explains that an empath:

Begin by taking a few, deep, long breaths. Then visualize a

beautiful shield of white or pink light completely surrounding your body and extending a few inches beyond it. This shield protects you from anything negative, stressful, toxic, or intrusive. Within the protection of this shield, feel yourself centered, happy, and energized. This shield blocks out negativity, but at the same time, you can still feel what's positive and loving. (Orloff, n.d.)

As with anything Shielding Visualization requires practice to master but it is an excellent tool for an empath just learning to protect their energy. There will still be many moments when an empath needs to place their shield up but are still growing accustomed to the practice. If an empath finds themselves getting anxious or tired in a public setting, they must use that as a reminder that their shield is down and to put it up. This practice will get easier with time but is effective especially for a beginner with no prior knowledge on shielding their energy.

An empath also needs to be proactive in protecting their energy. Shielding Visualization is an excellent tool for in the moment, but other things can help prevent the effects of being drained. Dr. Orloff, an empath herself, offers several tips for preventing, "empathy overload." To release negative energy, place a drop of lavender essential oil between your eyebrows or take a moment to simply inhale the scent and take deep calming breaths. Spending time in nature is another way to decompress and recharge. Furthermore it is extremely important for an empath to balance their alone time with their people time. (Orloff, n.d.)

In addition Dr. Orloff stresses the importance of time management skills. An empath needs to structure their day for success and recognize that they may need to be flexible in order to perform needed self care. During their weekend or personal time they should not plan too many things. Boundaries and keeping them are essential to an empath's survival. Personal boundaries include something like taking a break, to take deep breathes, or excusing themselves when anxiety begins to creep up. (Orloff, n.d.)

Dr. Orloff has termed draining people as "energy vampires," and stresses that empaths need to set clear and precise boundaries with them. Empaths need to stop explaining, be firm and resolved that, "No," is a complete sentence, nothing more needs to be said. Canceling plans is often difficult for an empath, however, this is vital and truly a skill needed for when an empath feels drained and needs to prioritize rest. Making plans for after work is great but they must not feel obligated to keep them if they feel drained by the end of shift. "I'm sorry I have to cancel," is enough of an explanation and no one else is entitled to someone else's time or energy. (Orloff, n.d.)

Setting boundaries is an obnoxiously hard skill for an empath to acquire and practicing self-compassion can help an empath affirm and prioritize their needs. After a hard day an empath may need to tell themselves, "I did the best I can, and the best is the best anyone can do," or "I did well, I have earned a break." Empaths naturally encourage and extend grace to others, however, they find it very difficult to extend themselves the same courtesy. For an empath to thrive they need to recognize that their energy needs to be protected and that no one else deserves their energy more than they do. (Orloff, n.d.)

An empath can also learn ways of protecting their energy within their environment. Creating environmental boundaries in the work place can be something like placing a plant or figurine between you and the next cubicle, or bringing in pictures of loved ones and keeping them in view. Another thing that an empath can try is finding ways to help them tune out the things happening in their environment. Essentially creating a mini sanctuary. This can be as simple as playing soft calming music, using noise canceling headphones, or even diffusing calming and rejuvenating essential oils. (Orloff, n.d.)

In her blog, 5 Protection Strategies for Empaths, Dr. Orloff advises that:

> As a sensitive person you must learn how to deal with sensory overload when too much is coming at you too quickly. This can leave you exhausted, anxious, depressed, or sick. Like many of us, you may feel there is no on/off switch for your empathy. This is not true. When you feel protected and safe you can take charge of your sensitivities rather than feeling victimized by them. To gain a sense of safety, recognize some common factors that contribute to empathy overload. Begin to identify your triggers. Then you can quickly act to remedy a situation. (Orloff, n.d.)

For an empath, self-discovery helps to identify where their energy is being taken and strategize how to protect it in the future. An empath's energy may be a gift that is meant to be shared but when and how should always be a conscious choice. Protecting and building their energy up is a giant step in harnessing the power of what it means to be an empath.

# Discovering Confidence and Purpose

Climate change, social unrest, political strife, disease, hunger, and thirst, are wreaking havoc on our world today. Most of these problems are propagated by selfishness. I believe that empaths are a gift, let's say from the universe, to help bring balance and harmony to this miserable and broken world. An empath's unique connection to the world, although not rare, is greatly needed to bridge the gap of disassociation. The majority of the world isn't attuned with the steady and constant information around us. On the contrary empaths are not only able to make these connections but an empath can also interpret their meaning and find their solutions.

Empaths by nature are very creative and think deeply. While the rest of the world is hung up on trying to make sense of issues an empath can often read the situation and identify the true core problem. An empath's ability to read and interpret energy is an asset to every situation. The empath that has learned to protect their own energy can often function as a mediator between surrounding energy and others. This can bring clarity to any given situation. Families, individuals, offices, governments, and our environment would all benefit from the influence of an empath.

Empaths need to realize that there is nothing wrong with them but rather they are greatly needed. Each empath is wired for gathering and interpreting energy or information but that does not mean they are all wired the same. There are certain energies that each empath or sensitive person is more comfortable or attuned with. Some empaths are better able to understand how animals feel and how to help them. Another may be more attuned to people, yet another finds their strongest connection to nature. The world needs thriving empaths; empaths that are able to freely share their gift. An empath can be confident that for this world to find healing, they are needed.

Although, the world seems to be set in order to control and obliterate an empath's gifting, this same world is screaming for a savior. One empath cannot be that savior, but an empath fulfilling their part and finding their meaning can make an incredible impact. Imagine what our world could be if 20% of the population was working to solve problems and facilitate healing.

That is a world worth pursuing and it is my hope that this chapter motivates and inspires empaths to realize their importance and take the steps necessary to heal and become a thriving empath. When an empath has allowed their gift to thrive it is the gift that keeps on giving. A thriving empath is able to mitigate problems and bring understanding to others.

# A reason to Thrive

In recent years there has been more awareness and tolerance built around the highly sensitive and empathic. However, exploring the possibility of being an empath is often met with resistance. The assumption that an empath relies on mysticism, superstitions, and folklore is a deterrent for many. Explaining an empath often comes across as illogical or reaching, an attempt to merely explain social anxiety or awkwardness. For older and unaware empaths, the notion of being highly sensitive or an empath, may initially be rejected. But when broken down into its simplest components, an empath simply has the ability to receive and interpret energy or information. It is more like information processing as opposed to magic.

Because the ability of an empath is at a disadvantage when trying to develop in a world that doesn't understand: Confusion, sickness, fatigue, and anxiety are all common attributes that an empath struggles with. When they are unable to understand their gifting and how to care for it these symptoms can dominate their life. Being attuned with everything around them an empath often finds it difficult to set boundaries and perform self-care. Moreover an empath is usually so hyper-focused on others that looking within does not align with their natural instincts to care for and help others. It is important to recognize that the desire to help simply comes with the territory of being an empath. But a worn out, sick, anxious and drained individual is very limited in what they can do or accomplish, empath or not.

The gift of high sensitivity or being an empath often tries to signal an empath that there is more going on than just fatigue, or social anxiety. Empaths tend to be naturally curious and inquisitive, but the common misconceptions and labels that an empath accepts in order to try and explain their behavior often inhibit them from being able to find answers. However once an empath is willing to accept that they may just gather and process information or energy differently then the real work begins. Many empaths need to heal from the consequences of not understanding their gift. An empath often feels drained because their energy is literally drained out of them. Depending on how ingrained certain habits and practices are will often determine the amount of time and energy an empath needs to heal. Reversing the side-effects of misunderstanding is greatly needed for an empath to be able to stop being reactive and begin to be proactive.

An empath needs to take specific steps to not only heal but unlock their natural ability to communicate and exchange with the world around them. The steps necessary for an empath to thrive requires a lot of forethought, insight, and determination. The investment of time and energy may seem unequal to the resulting energy produced but in time that investment will more than pay off.

An empath must create space between them and the things draining their energy. To protect their energy an empath needs to learn how to shield their energy from being drained. Self-care is essential for an empath to allow their energy to recharge and this may take significant time and planning. By protecting and recharging their energy an empath can then begin to heal physically, mentally, and emotionally. This process may take more time for some than others depending on how exhausted and drained they are. An empath must be diligent in shielding and protecting their energy until they are able to reach a point of restoration. An empath needs to be able to harness and focus their energy to be able to help others and restoration is the key required for an empath to begin to share their gift and experience fulfillment.

If you suspect or have recently discovered you are an empath then you must learn how to protect and harness this gift. Science class teaches us that energy can never be created or destroyed, it can only change forms. Applying this concept we can say that an empath or highly sensitive person is adept at perceiving energy and energy transfers. Energy has many forms and the ability to pick up on specific energy signatures take on just as many forms.

When an empath is able to figure out what energy exchanges they are more attune with then finding their purpose is the natural next step. For example if an empath is more attune with animals then pursuing endeavors around animals and their protection or conservation makes perfect sense. If a person is more attune with people and work dynamics then perhaps starting a consulting business for employers is what is needed. Becoming familiar with how they best receive and process energy and information an empath is able to discover how their unique gifting is meant to serve and heal.

There are many concepts that seem counter-intuitive for an empath to accept and begin the journey to healing and purpose. Although safeguarding their energy may feel unnatural, it is necessary for an empath to learn the skills needed. Recognizing how they can take action and serve a greater purpose is important for an empath to thrive. The world needs empaths to be who they are meant to be. In their ideal state an empath can experience how freeing and rewarding their gift can be.

A thriving empath is able to distinguish how they receive and interpret energy. Finding satisfaction in serving with the energy they best understand they can literally change the world. A thriving empath has not only harnessed the ability to overcome and heal themselves but empowered their gift to bring healing and balance around them. When an empath is able to freely share their gift they fulfill the greater purpose of playing an essential part in restoring balance to a broken and miserable world.

## *To conclude*

The common plight of an empath or highly sensitive individual may seem dire but the ability to overcome is taking the steps necessary to begin looking within. Learning that there is a reason for the way they are is the beginning, deciding to embark on a journey to self-discovery is a difficult choice and there is a great deal of work ahead. For an empath the realization that what sets them apart can easily be explained brings a sense of relief and sometimes euphoria. Despite the hardships that may accompany the gift of being an empath it is never too late to learn how to harness its power.

Self-discovery is important for an empath in order for them to understand how they operate. Creating space and allowing their own feelings to become their own is the first thing needed to begin this journey. Within this understanding is an ability to begin to heal, this process requires an empath to learn how to protect their energy and then recharge. This may take time but the results are unparalleled. Finally, an empath is ready to begin exploring and discovering their unique wiring and connections. Identifying these connections is enlightening and often energizing for an empath. As discovery grows an empath's personal purpose and meaning in life becomes clear. This enlightenment not only brings satisfaction and peace to an empath, it fills a need in a world starving for attention and care.

When unlocked the very nature of being an empath gifts and equips an empath with their own creativity and insight. These essential tools allow an empath to navigate through the hardships and problems of life. By embarking on the journey of self discovery; inner peace, healing, satisfaction and purpose are all obtainable for a struggling empath.

<h1 style="text-align:center">From a Grateful Heart</h1>

T he work and research of Dr. Judith Orloff, has especially been of help to me. Some of her works as well as others all made this book possible. The following are the resources I used for this specific production:

## References

Campbell, L. (2022, July 29). What Does It Mean to Be an Empath? Verywell Mind. Retrieved September 27, 2022, from https://www.verywellmind.com/what-is-an-empath-and-how-do-you-know-if-you-are-one-5119883

Garis, M. G. (2020, November 9). *There Are 8 Types of Empaths: and Only 1 Has to Do With Feeling the Emotions of Others.* Well+Good. Retrieved September 28, 2022, from https://www.wellandgood.com/types-of-empaths/

Li, P. MS, MBA. (2022, September 23). *Parenting Strategies That Help Your Highly Sensitive Child Thrive.* Parenting for Brain. Retrieved September

27, 2022, from https://www.parentingforbrain.com/highly-sensitive-child/

Orloff, J. M.D. (n.d.-a). 5 Protection Strategies for Empaths. *Judith Orloff M.D.* Retrieved September 29, 2022, from https://drjudithorloff.com/5-protection-strategies-for-empaths-2/

Orloff, J. M.D. (n.d.-a). *Top 10 Traits of an Empath. Judith Orloff* M.D. Retrieved September 28, 2022, from https://drjudithorloff.com/top-10-traits-of-an-empath/

# Conclusion

I hope you not only got what you needed out of this short read, but I also hope you enjoyed it, and if you did I encourage you to leave a favorable review. This is also my first book and I would love to hear what you think, you can email me at ansily2thePoint@outlook.com

Thank you for taking the time and energy to read this book, now go out and thrive!

# About the Author

Ansily has the honor and privilege of living in in the Pacific Northwest and enjoys the photography opportunities it provides. As an experienced tutor she is passionate about learning and sharing. She says, "As a new learner begins to understand, I love watching the excitement spark in their eyes." She lives a modest life in her home in Oregon and continuously looks for new endeavors and opportunities to grow and learn.

Ansily designed a simple 12 week prompt journal. This journal has the specific needs of an empath in mind but can be a resource or tool for any individual.

**Discovering your Why? 12 week Transformation for Healing Journal**

Only available on Amazon. A prompt journal with the needs of empaths in mind. Daily entries with a weekly check in prompts you to track your energy expenditures, find things you enjoy, look for meaningful interactions, celebrate self-driven accomplishments, as well as set goals for 12 weeks. This journal can help you change your patterns and prioritize healing. You'll be amazed at what an impact on your mental and physical health just paying attention can do.

www.ingramcontent.com/pod-product-compliance
Lightning Source LLC
Chambersburg PA
CBHW051723250726

48653CB00008B/3168